DINOJITSU

Submissions & Positions

Brazilian Jiu-Jitsu Coloring Book

Monkey Mount

COLLECT THE WHOLE DINOJITSU SERIES!

A word to grown-ups from Monkey Mount

Monkey Mount is a team of creatives and Jiu Jitsu practitioners with a common goal: *to inspire others*. This community was created by Brazilian Jiu-Jitsu and Judo Black Belt Yacinta Nguyen with the intent of inspiring her students to see the magic in the martial arts that have transformed her life.

Professor Yacinta Nguyen is among the elite Brazilian Jiu Jitsu practitioners in Canada. She holds accolades from the most prestigious competitions around the world and is also featured on the *BJJ Heroes* website. Moreover, her passion and focus now is to bring together the wonderful talent in the community and leverage Brazilian Jiu-Jitsu as a means to:

- empower our children through *confidence building* and *resilience training*
- show young girls that *strong is beautiful*
- improve *mental health* in the community

We hope you enjoy this coloring book as much as we enjoyed creating it. If you did, please consider taking a moment out of your busy day to leave us a review, this is more helpful than you can imagine and will allow us to keep on creating more books for the community.

With Love,

The Monkey Mount Team

JOIN OUR COMMUNITY ON SOCIAL MEDIA!

@MONKEYMOUNTBOOKS

oss

oss

ARMBAR

ARMBAR

SCARF HOLD

SCARF

HOLD

SCARF HOLD

REAR NAKED CHOKE

REAR NAKED CHOKE

BACK CONTROL

BACK CONTROL

BACK CONTROL

TRIANGLE

TRIANGLE

NORTH SOUTH

NORTH SOUTH

BOW AND ARROW

BOW AND ARROW

TURTLE

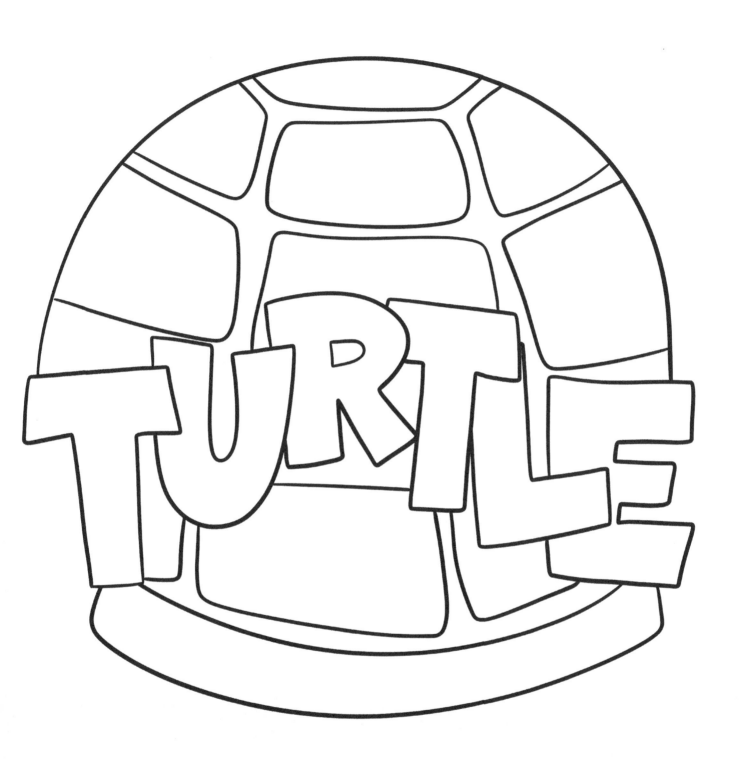

TURTLE

BASEBALL BAT CHOKE

BASEBALL
BAT
CHOKE

BASEBALL BAT CHOKE

SIDE CONTROL

SIDE CONTROL

SIDE CONTROL

KIMURA

KIMURA

KNEE ON BELLY

KNEE ON BELLY

NORTH SOUTH CHOKE

NORTH SOUTH CHOKE

MOUNT

MOUNT

AMERICANA

AMERICANA

Made in the USA
Las Vegas, NV
21 December 2023

83337717R00039